Chariot Coloring book

THOM BREAS

Copyright © 2020 Thom Breas

Todos los derechos reservados.

Copyright © 2020 Thom Breas

This book or any portion thereof may not be reproduced or used in any manner whatsoever without the express without the express written permission of the author or the Publisher.

By amazon.

INTRODUCTION

Tanks are the successors to war chariots and armored elephants used by armies of ancient times. Designed to be used as part of large infantry units, or as a separate striking force, the modern tank is a formidable weapon of war.

Tanks, are just some of the beautiful illustrations you will find in this coloring book.

The coloring style is novel and our unique designs will need your creativity to get inspiration with fabulous illustrations for your wall or your next artistic work.

This coloring book is made up drawings being perfect for colorists allowing the maximum performance of their abilities in the choice and combination of colors in a practical, relaxed and fun way.

When you start coloring, think about the drawing process and the colors and nothing else.

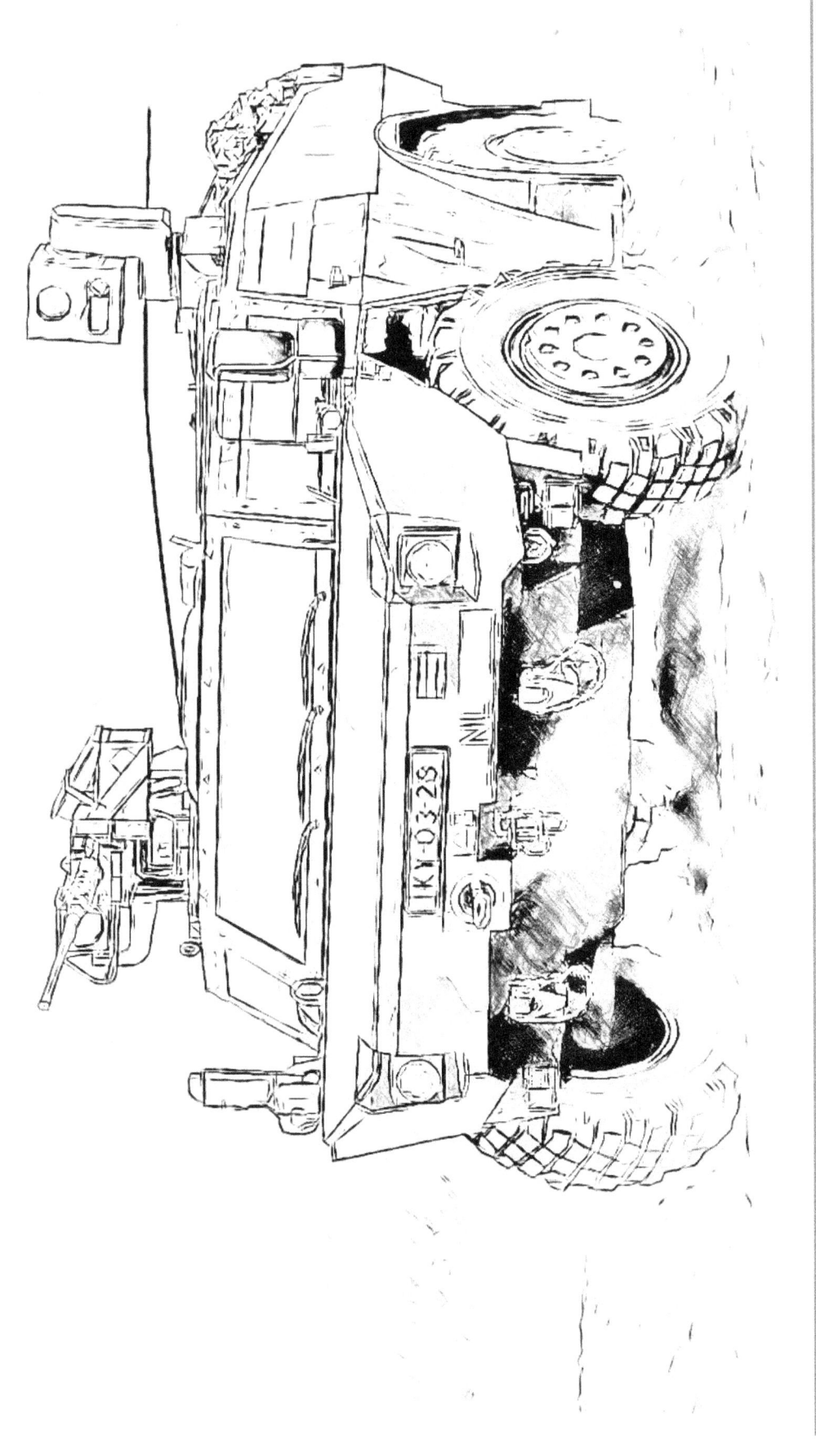

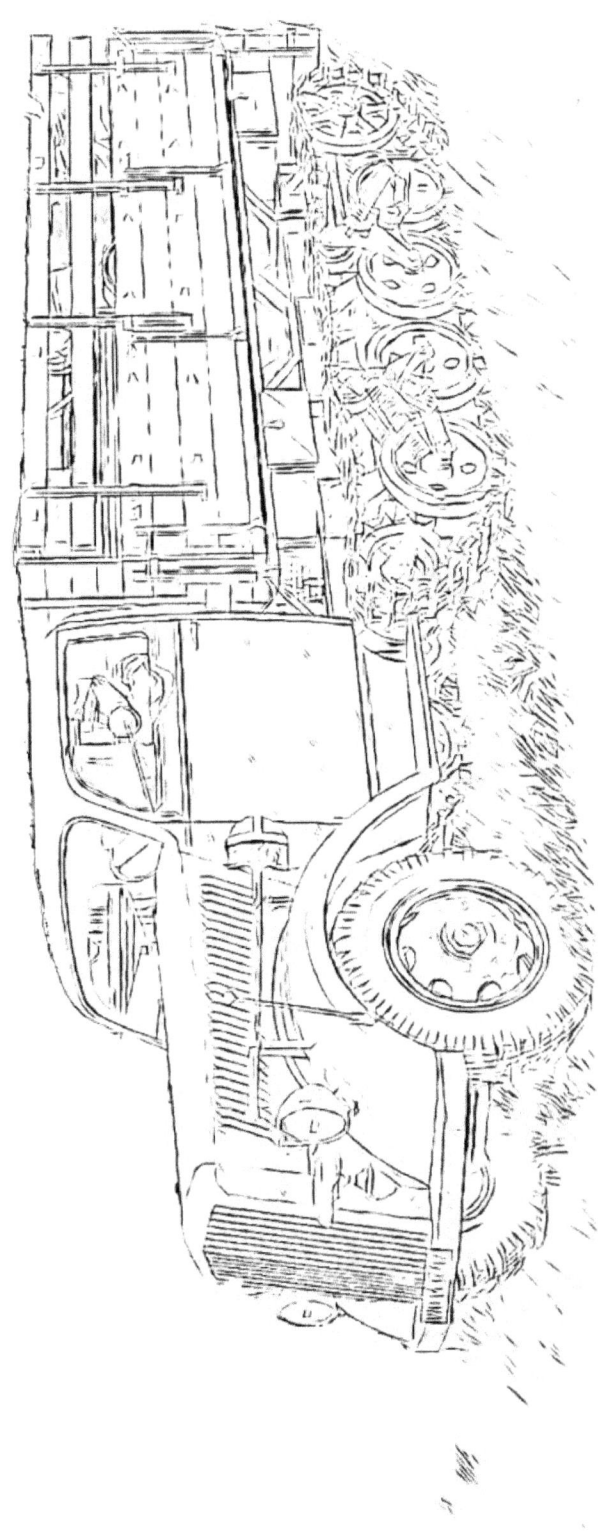

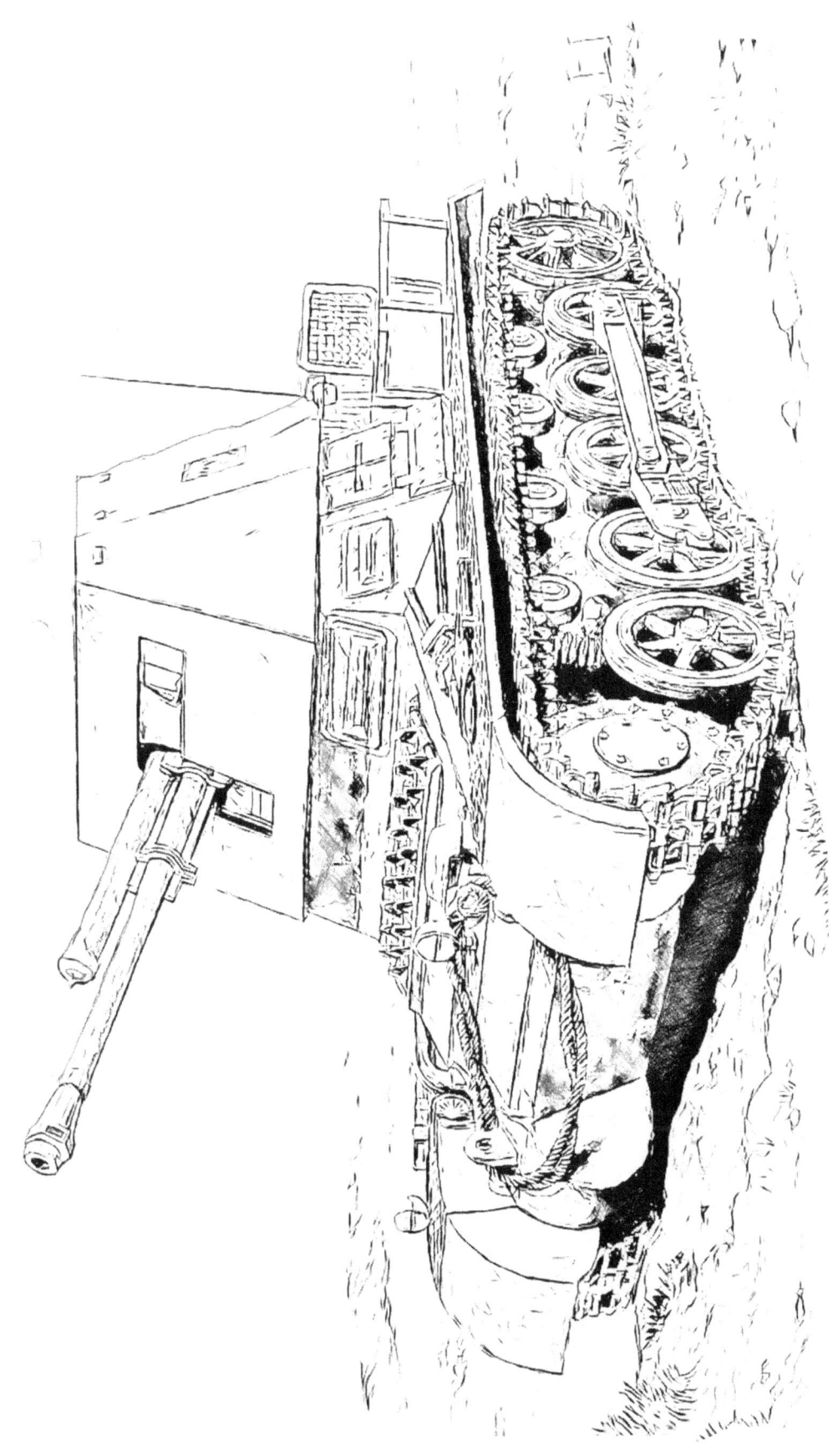

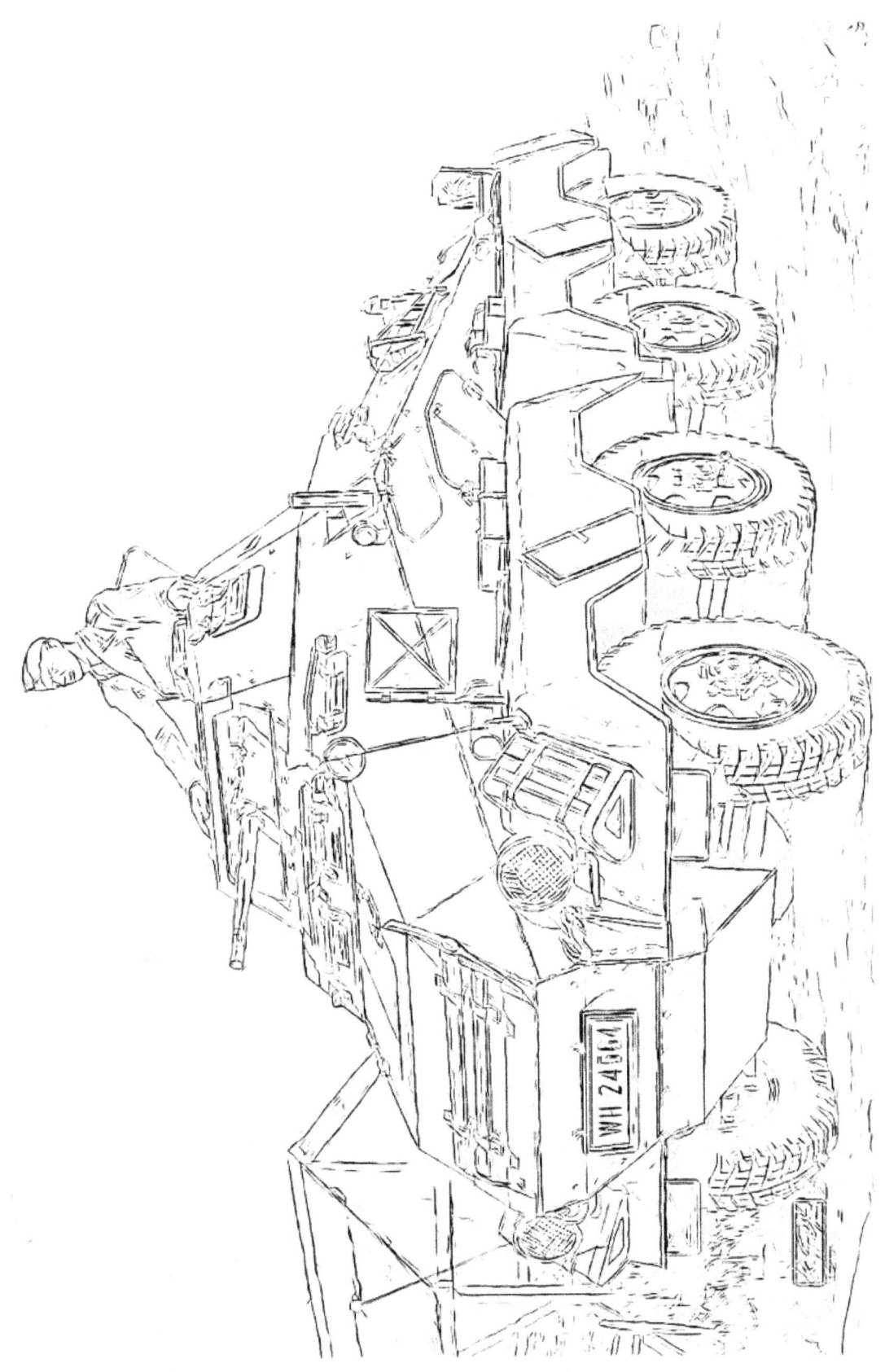

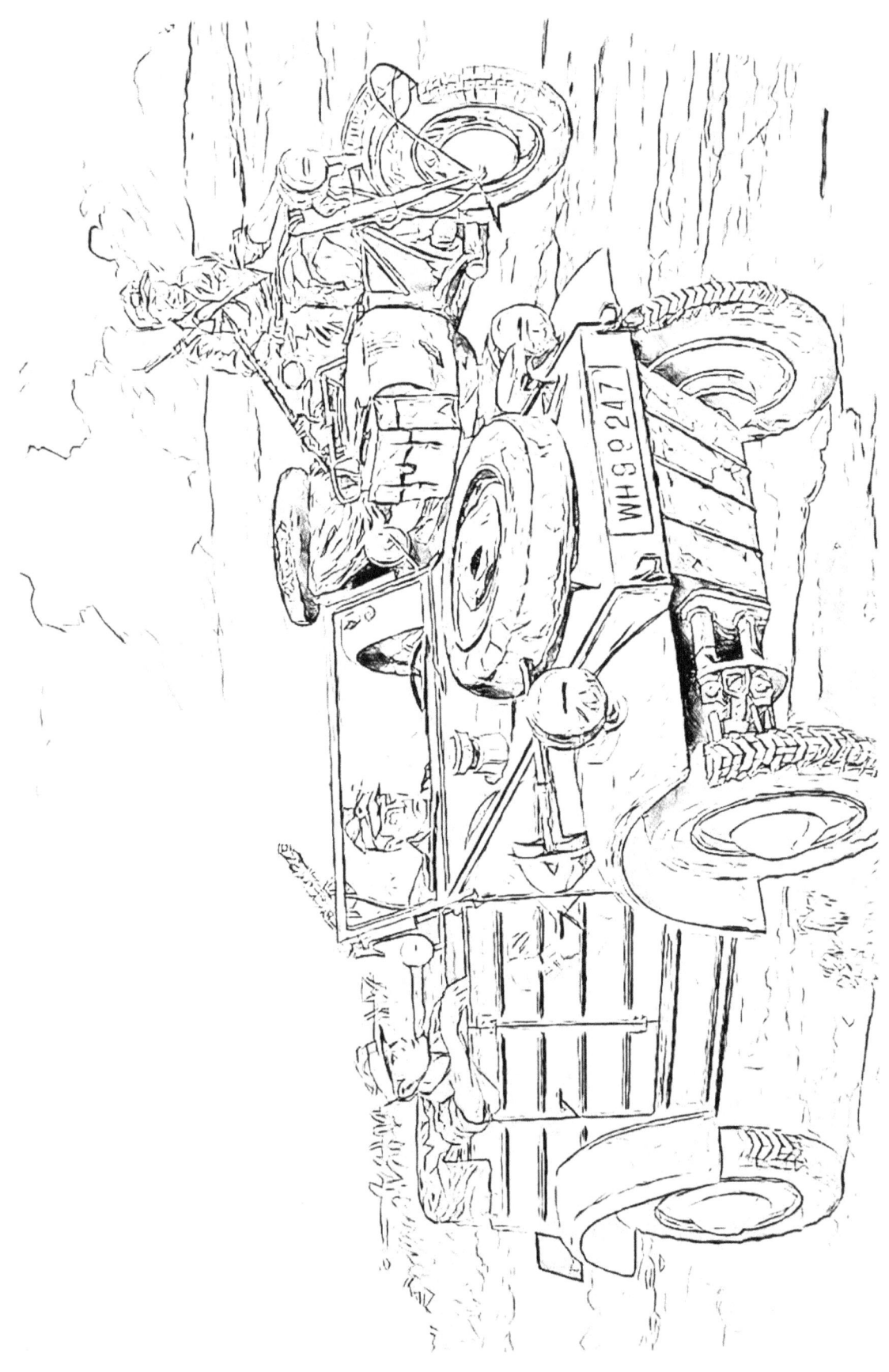

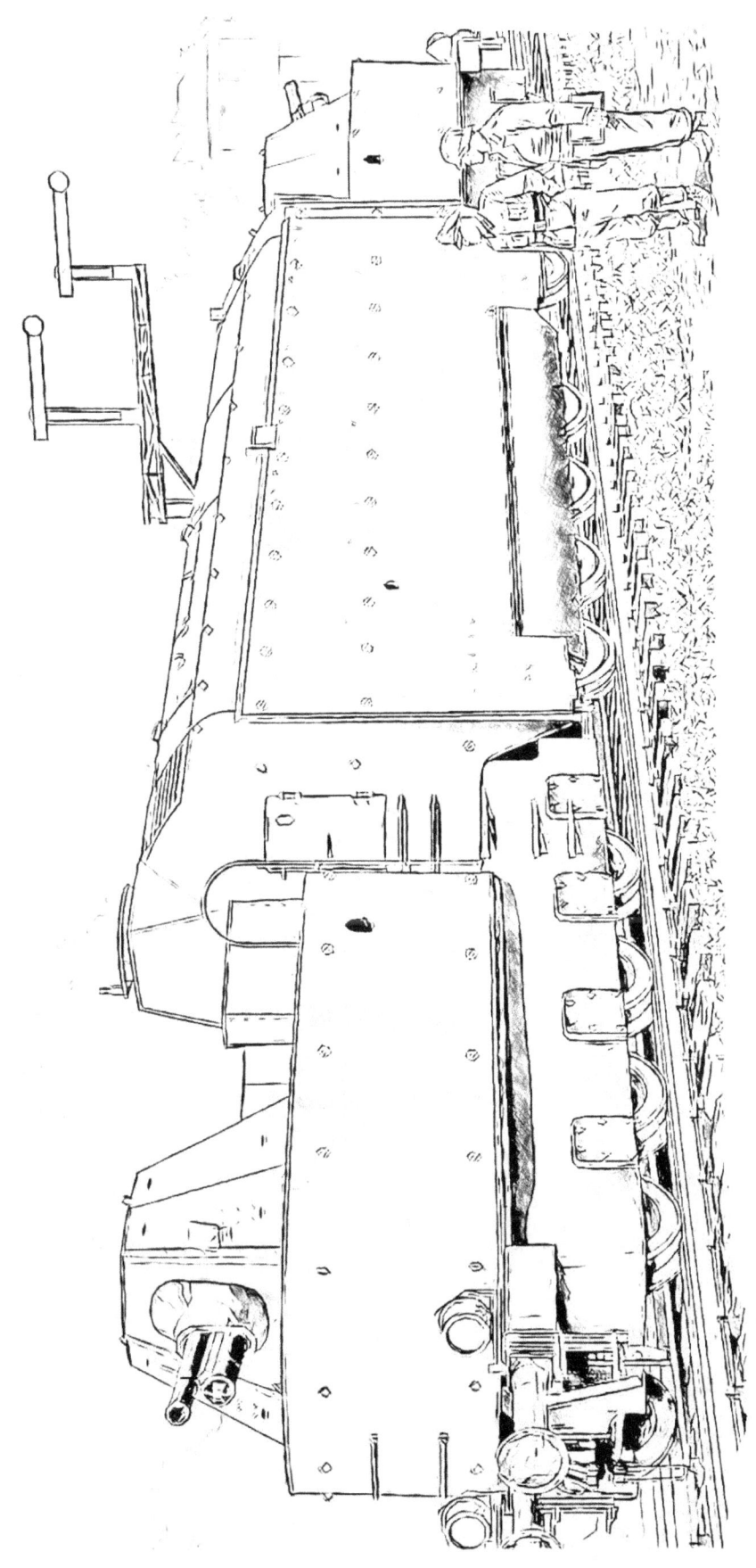

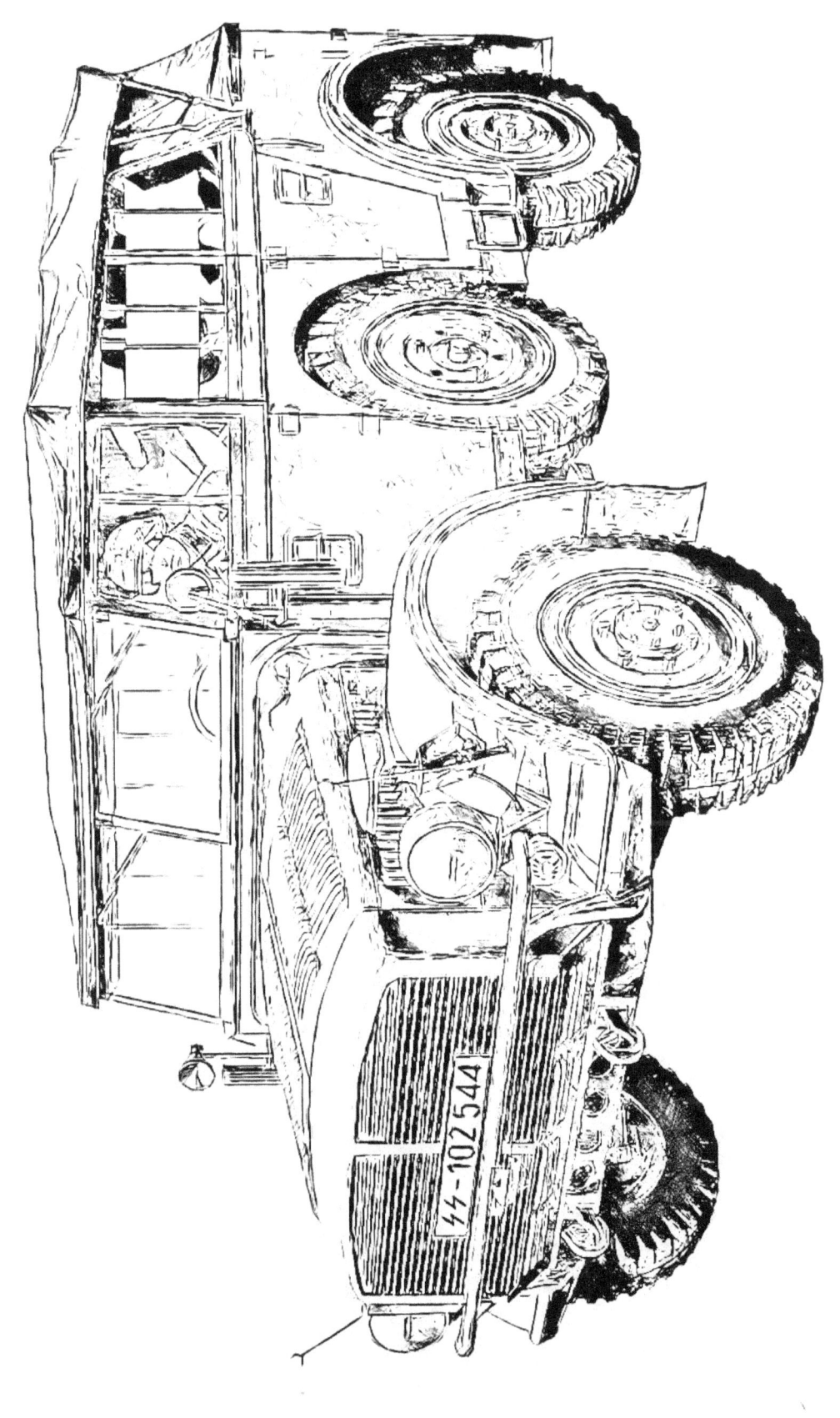

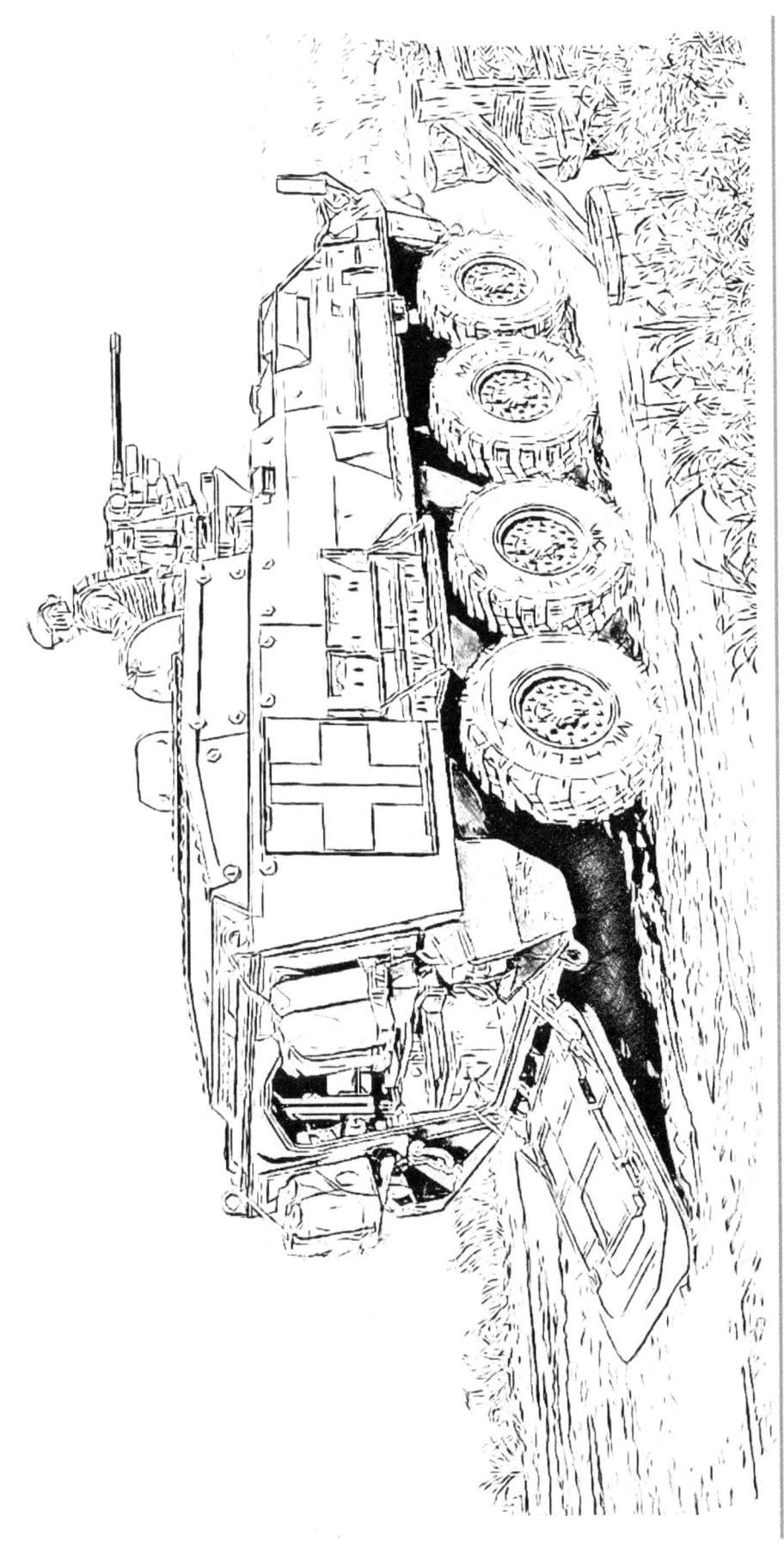

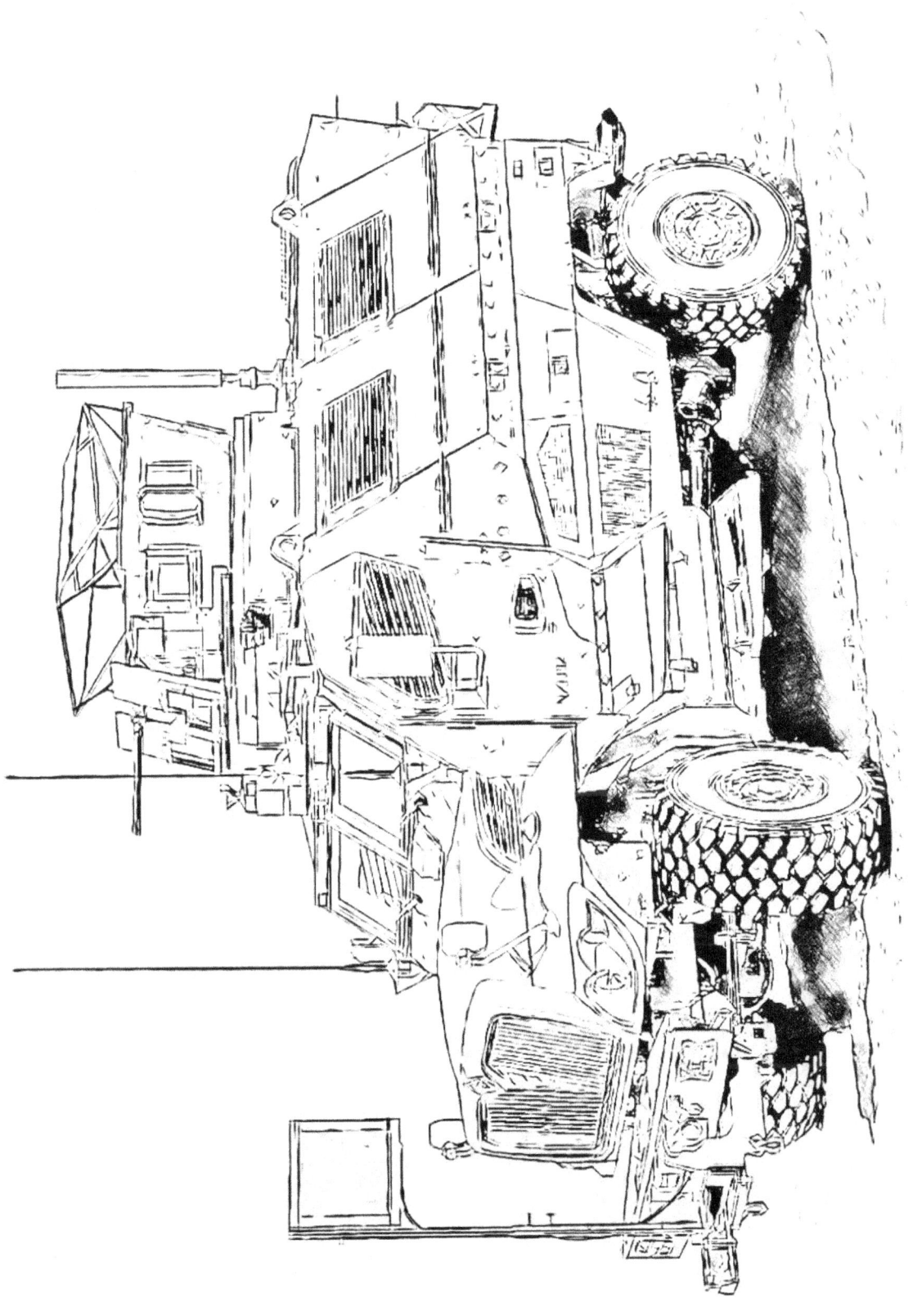

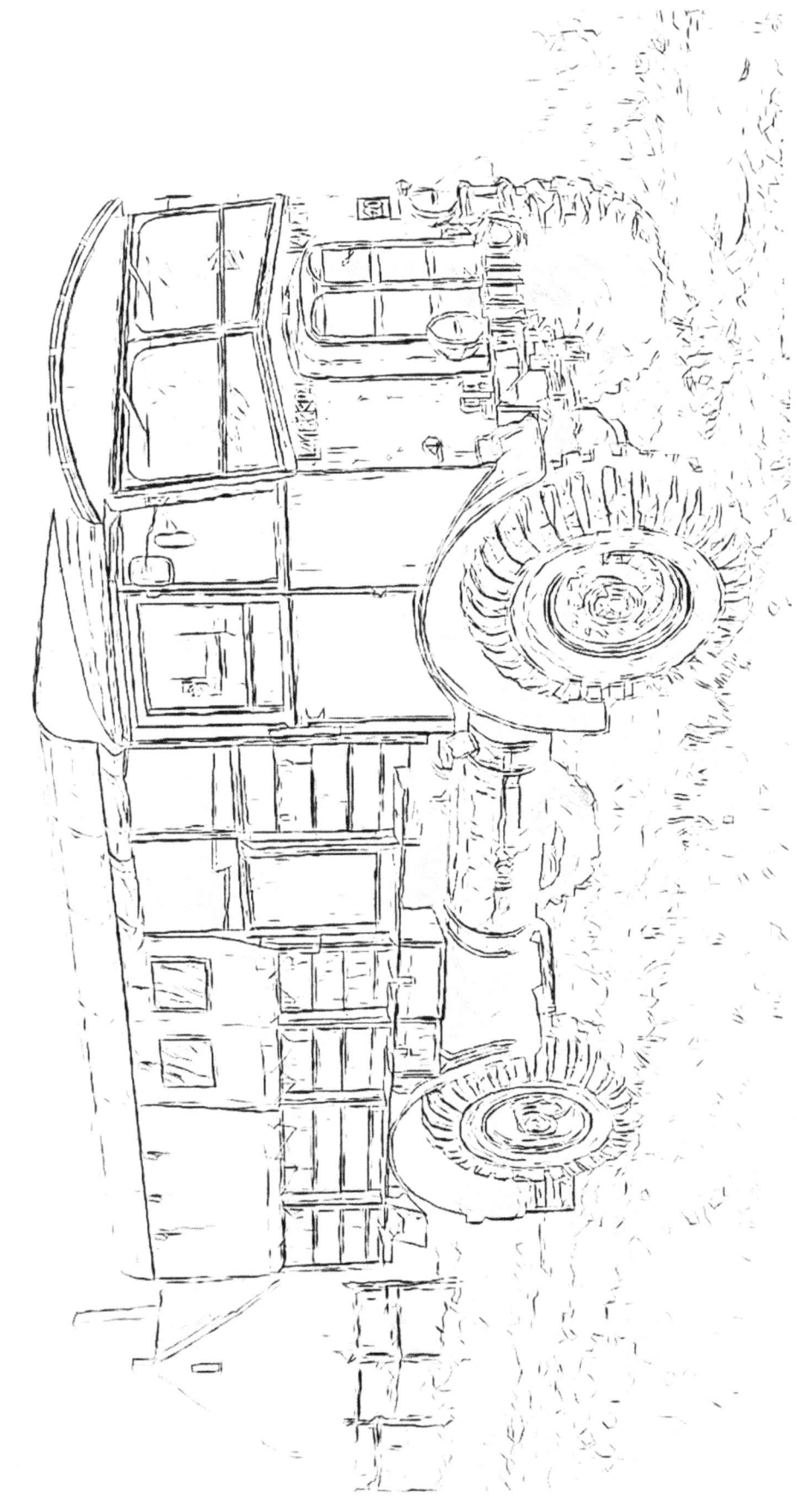

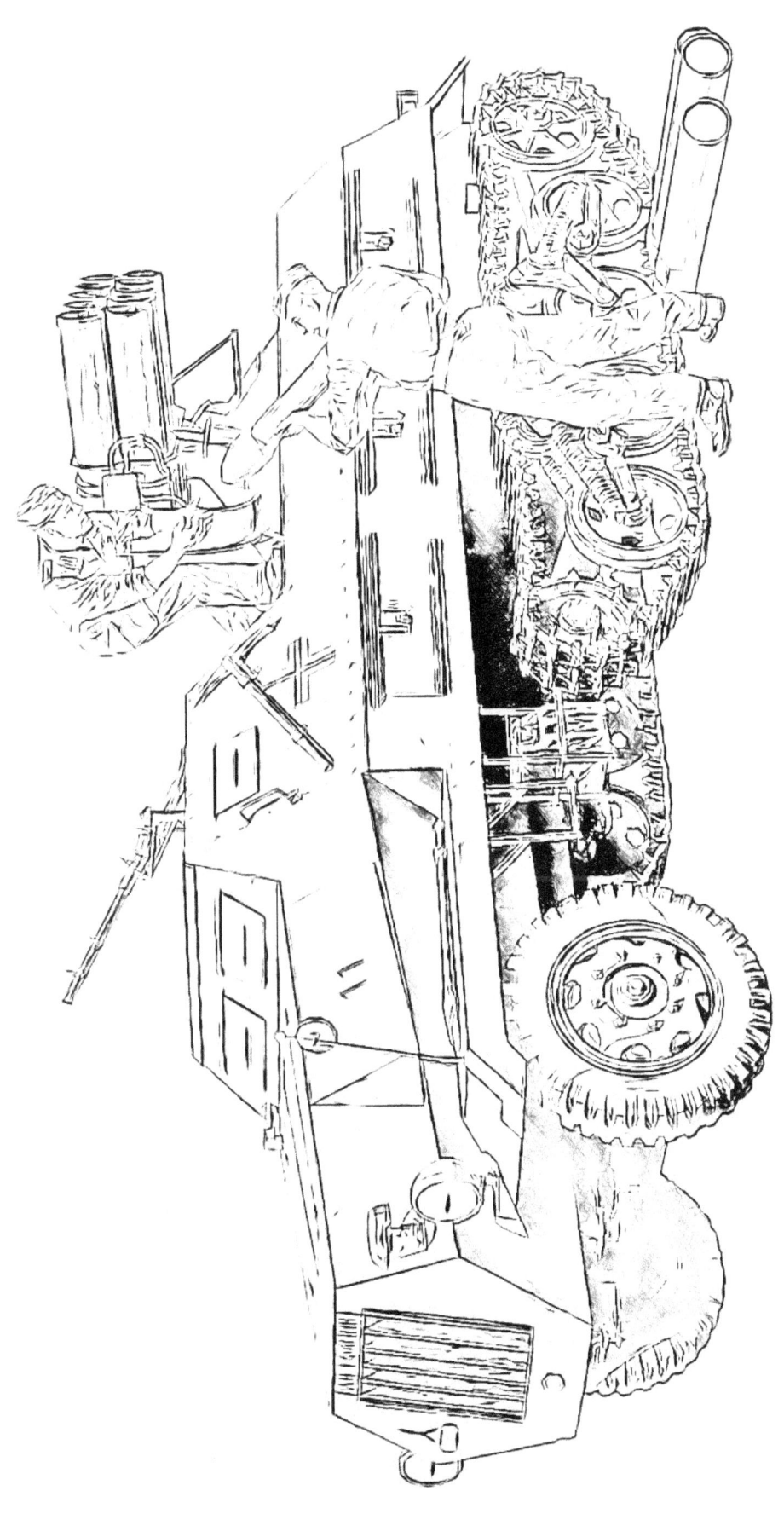

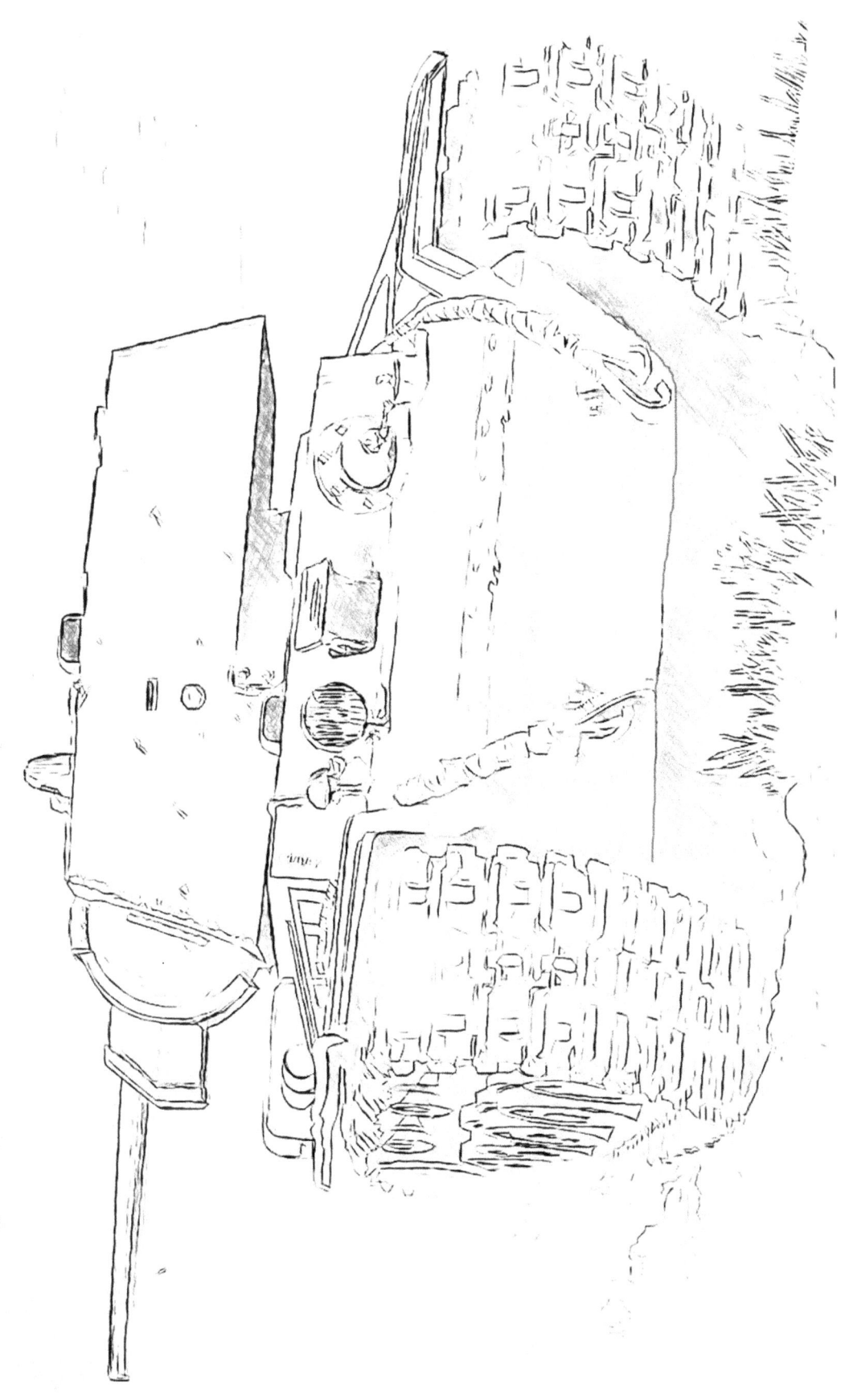

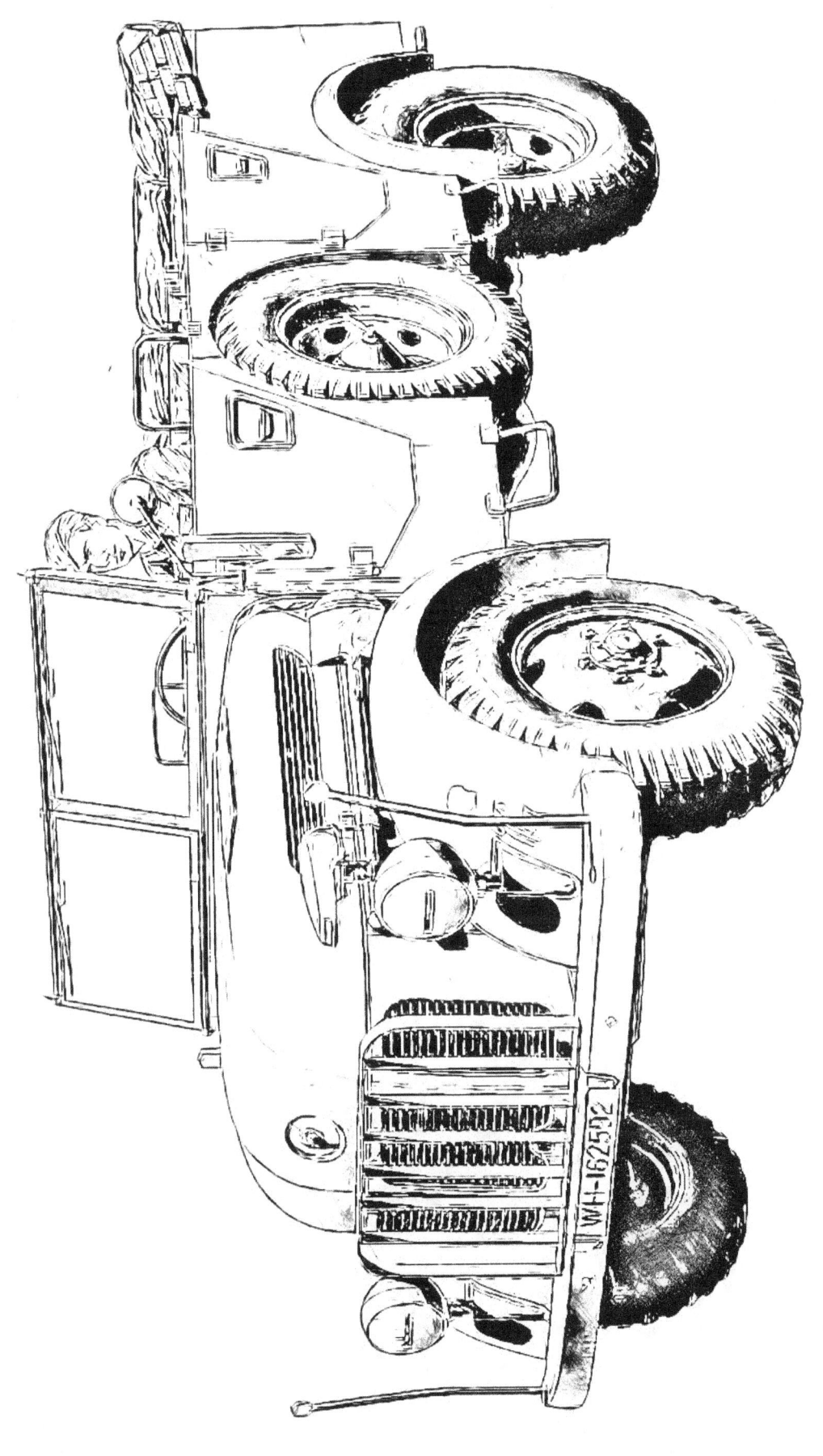

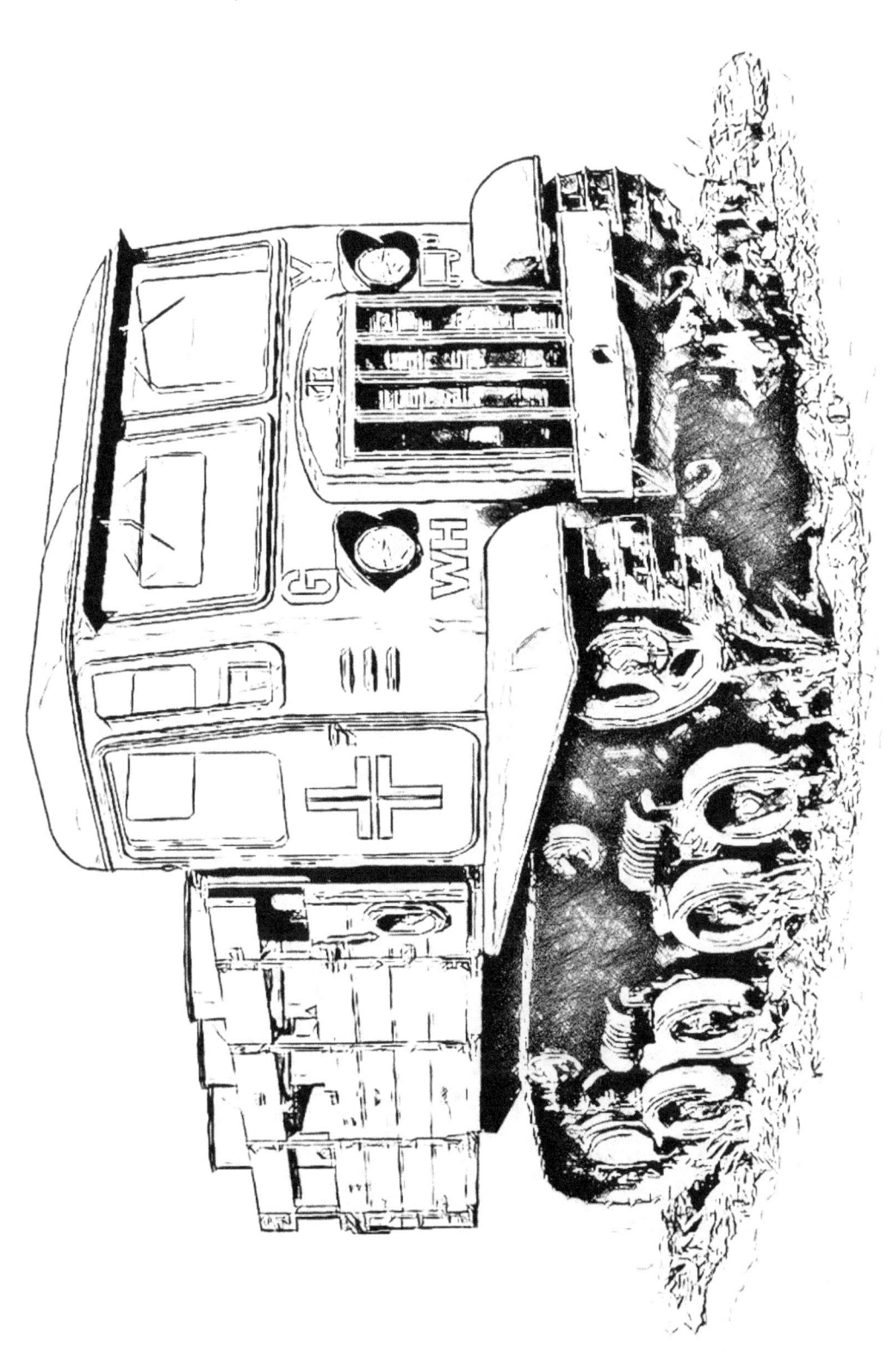

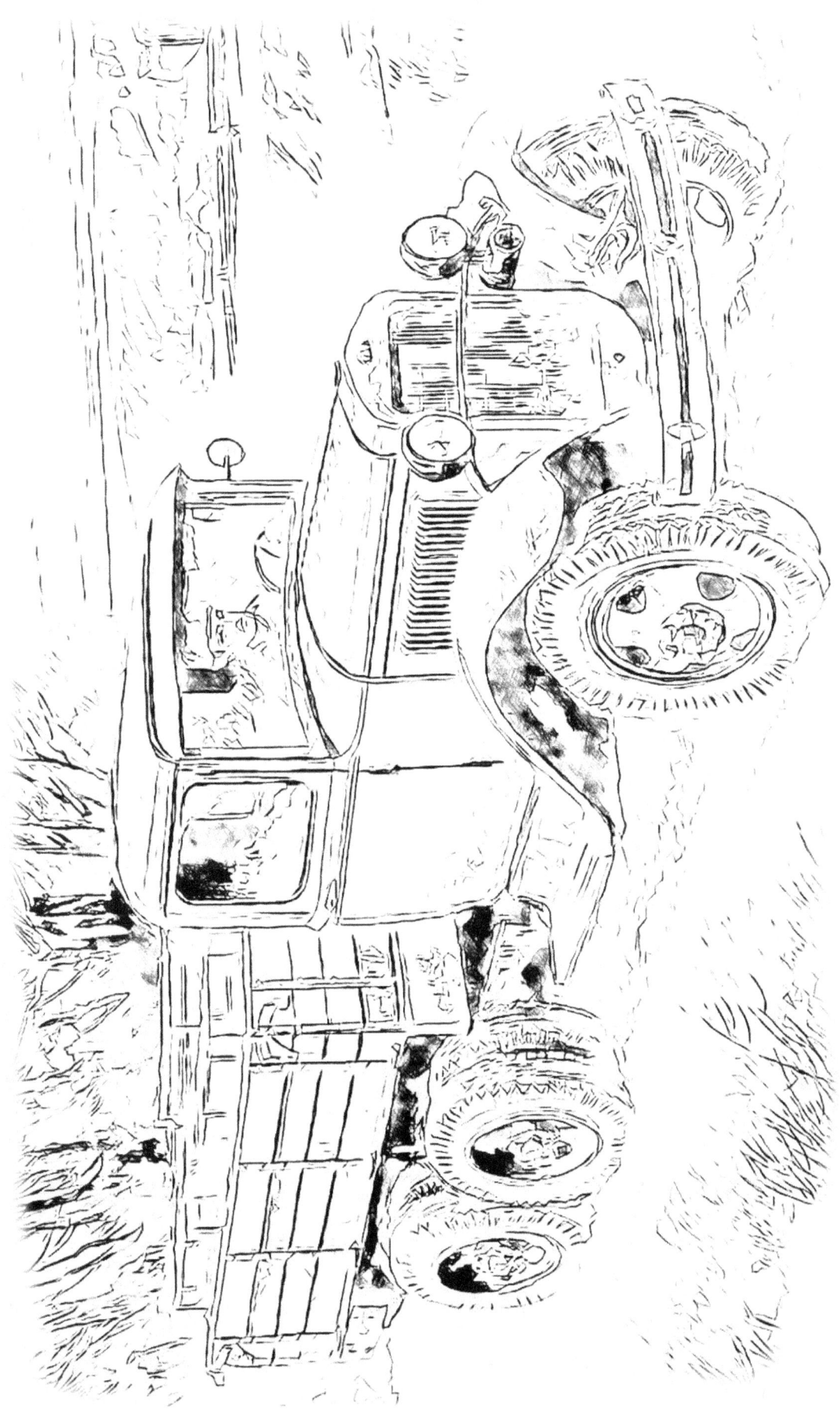

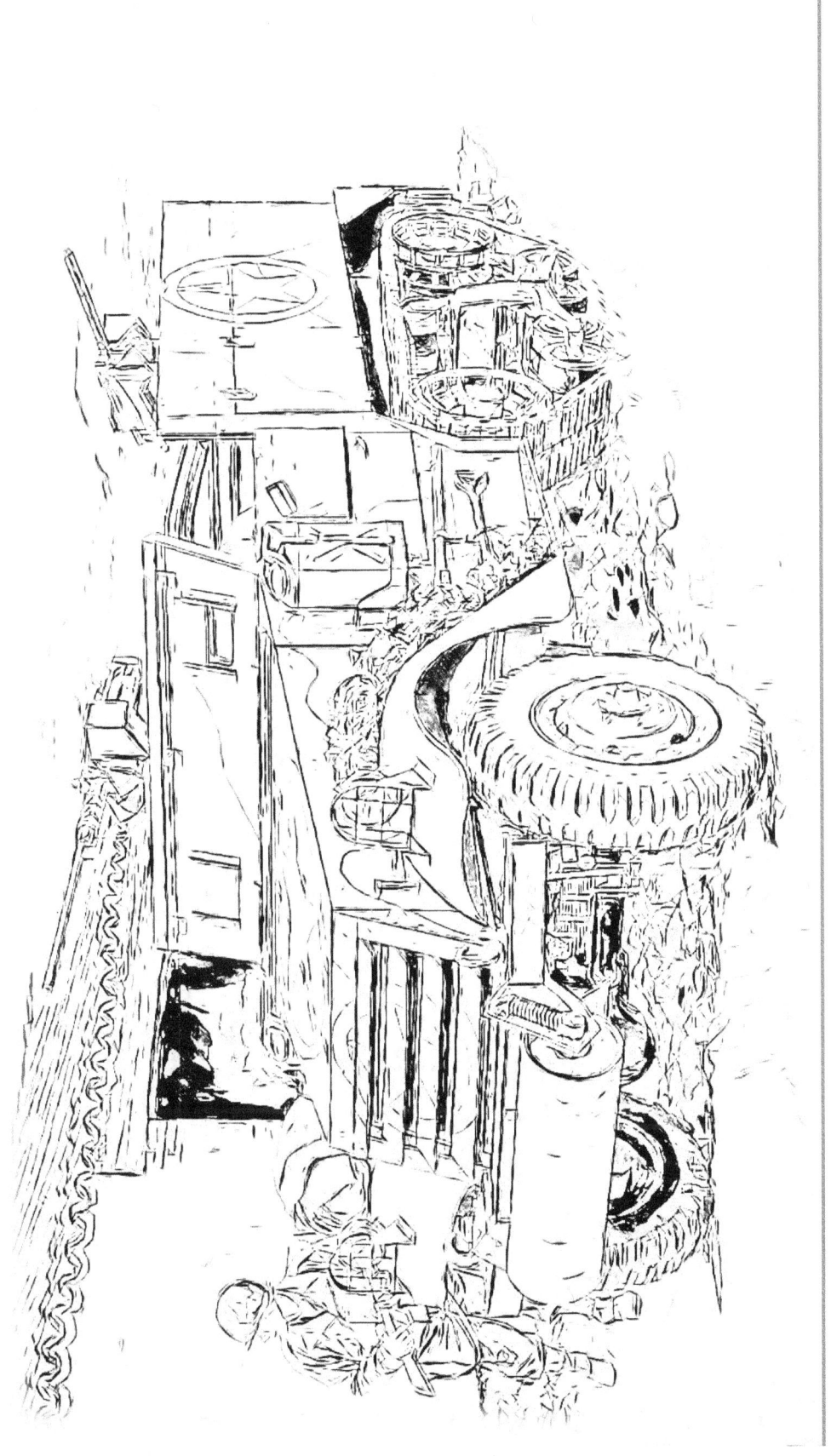

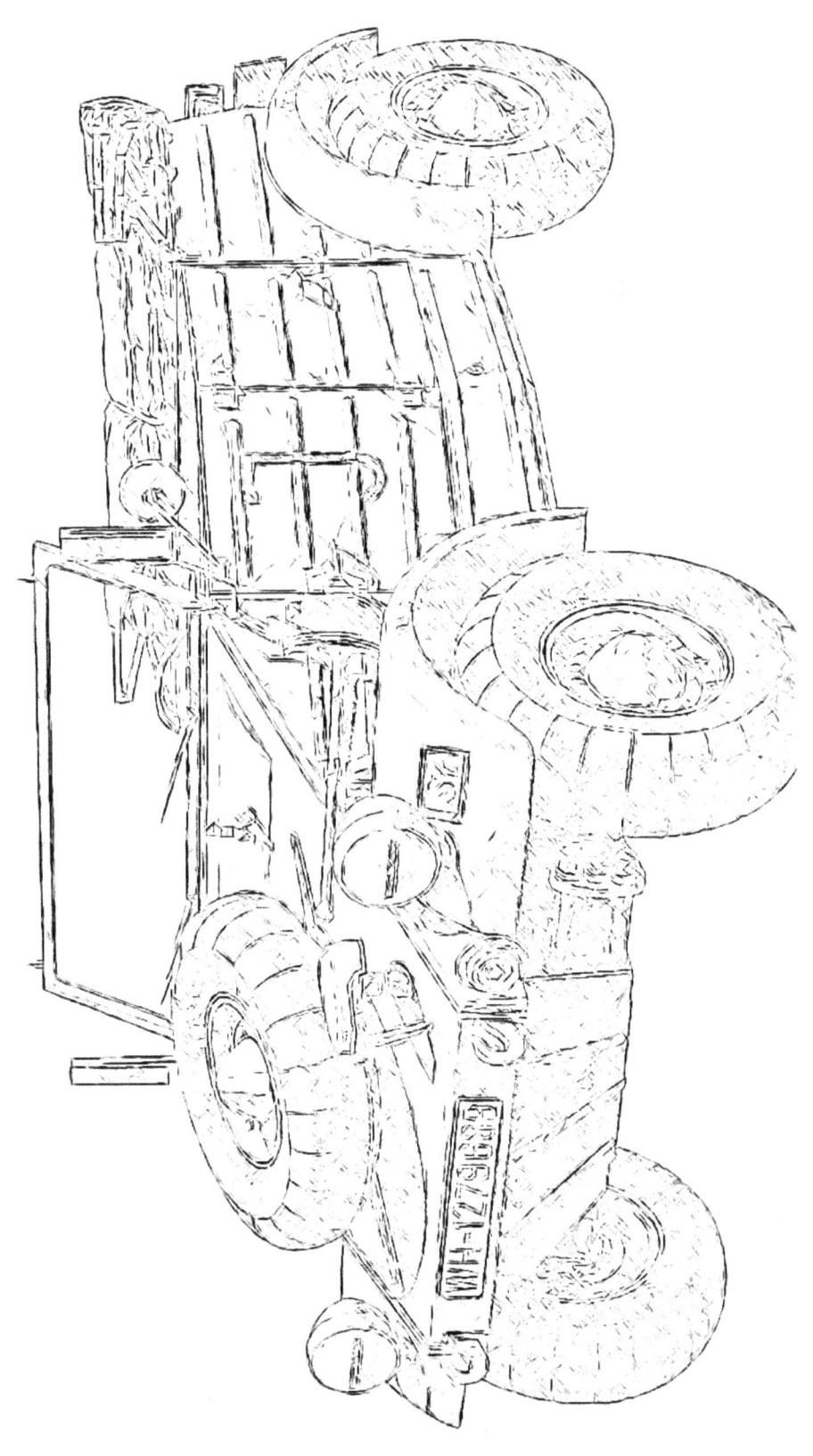

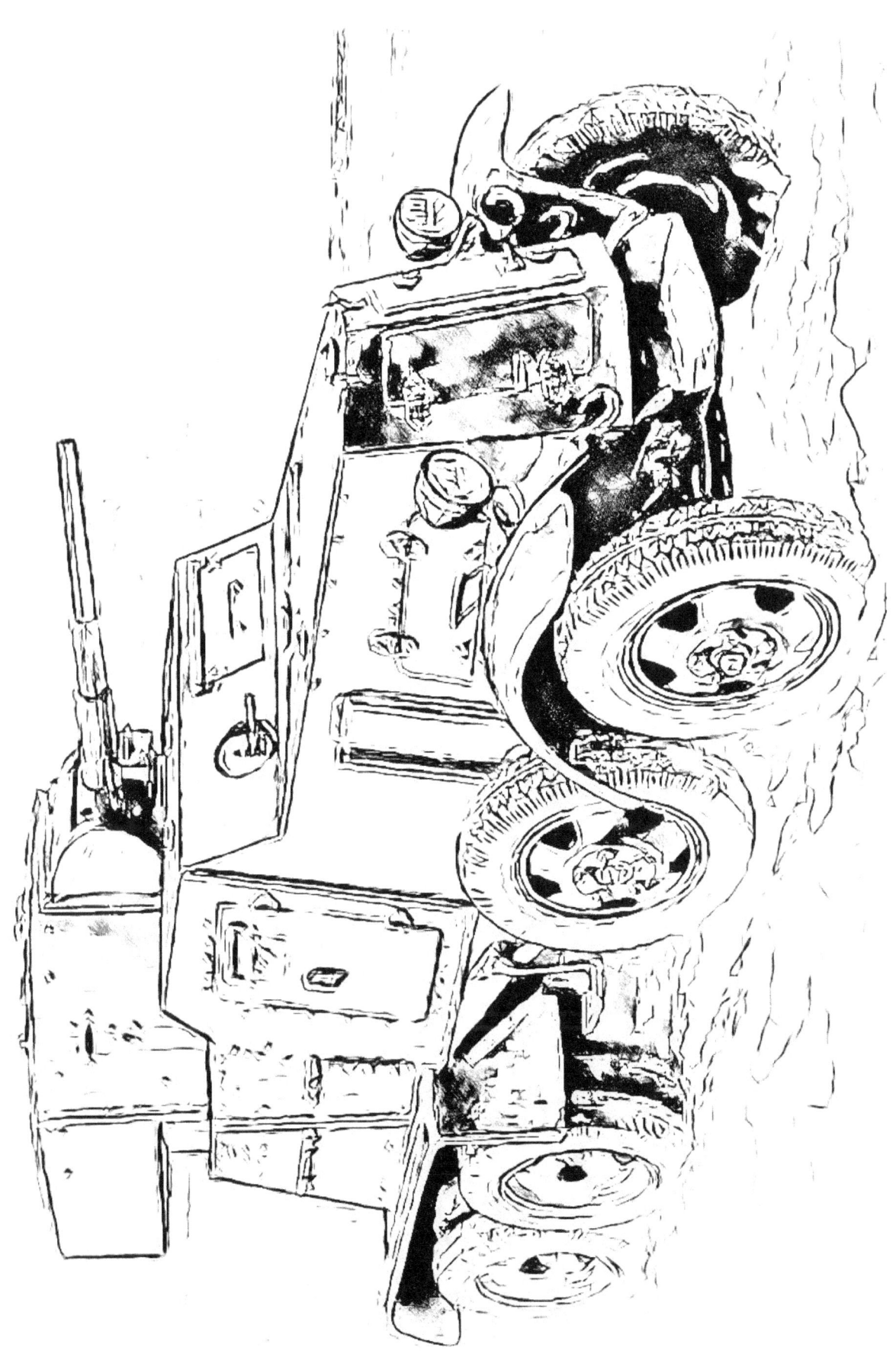

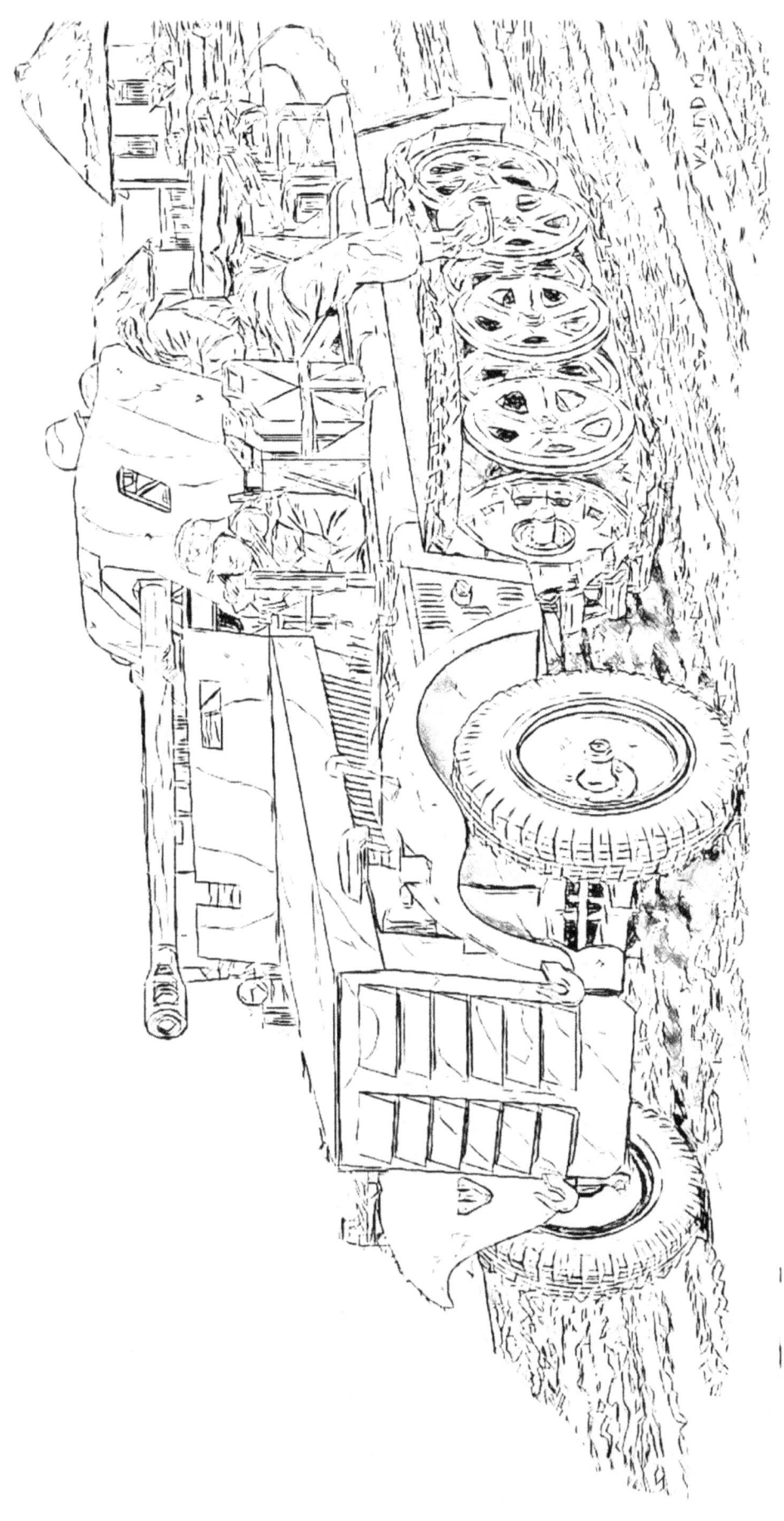

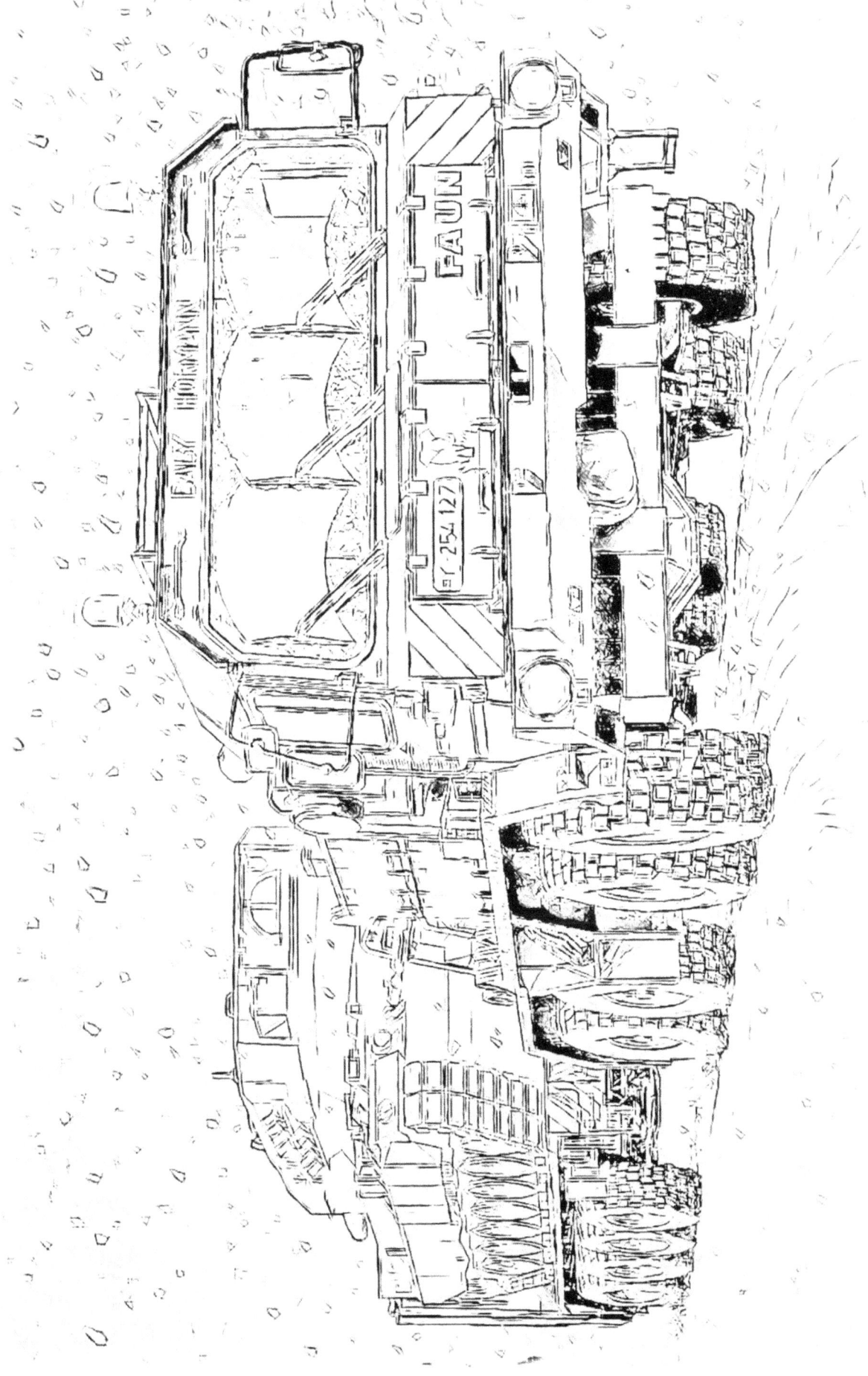

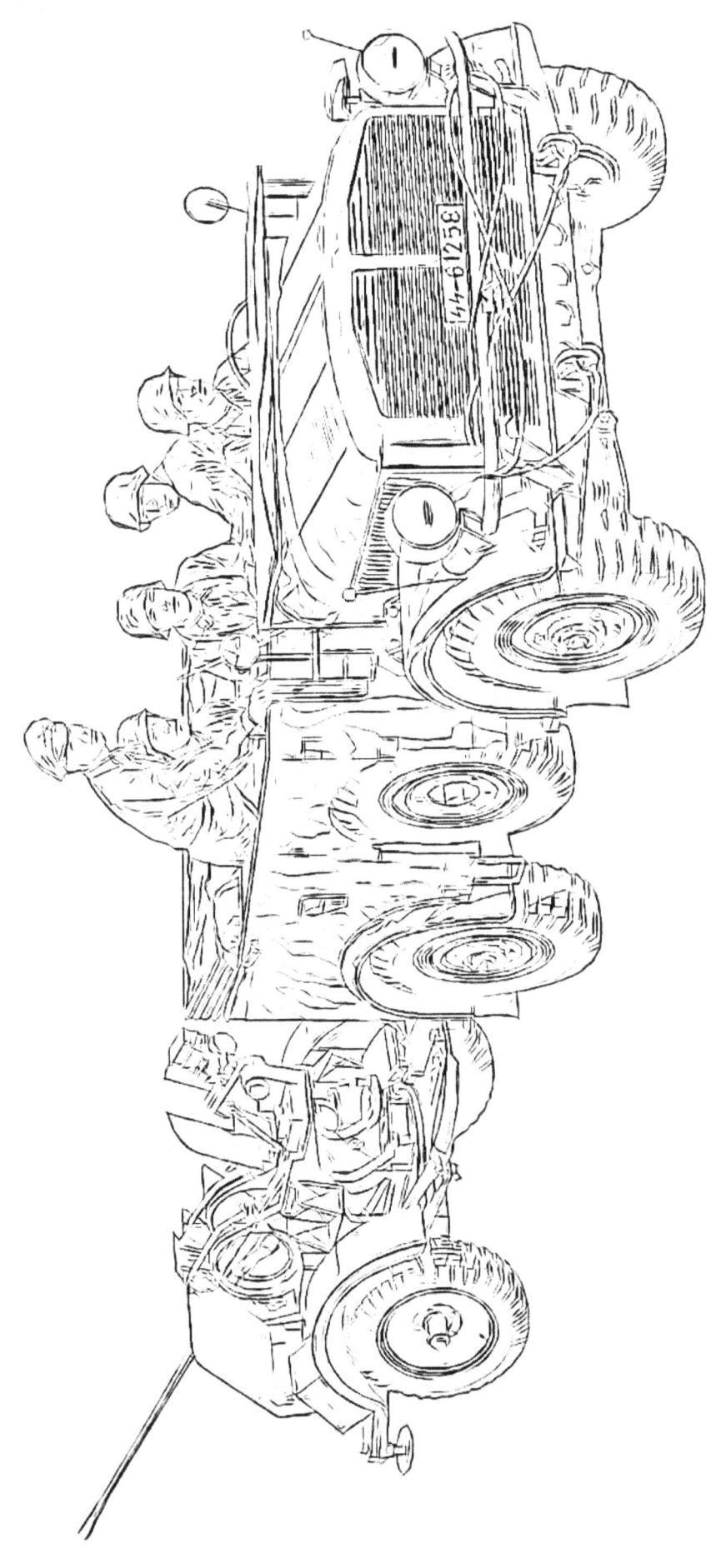

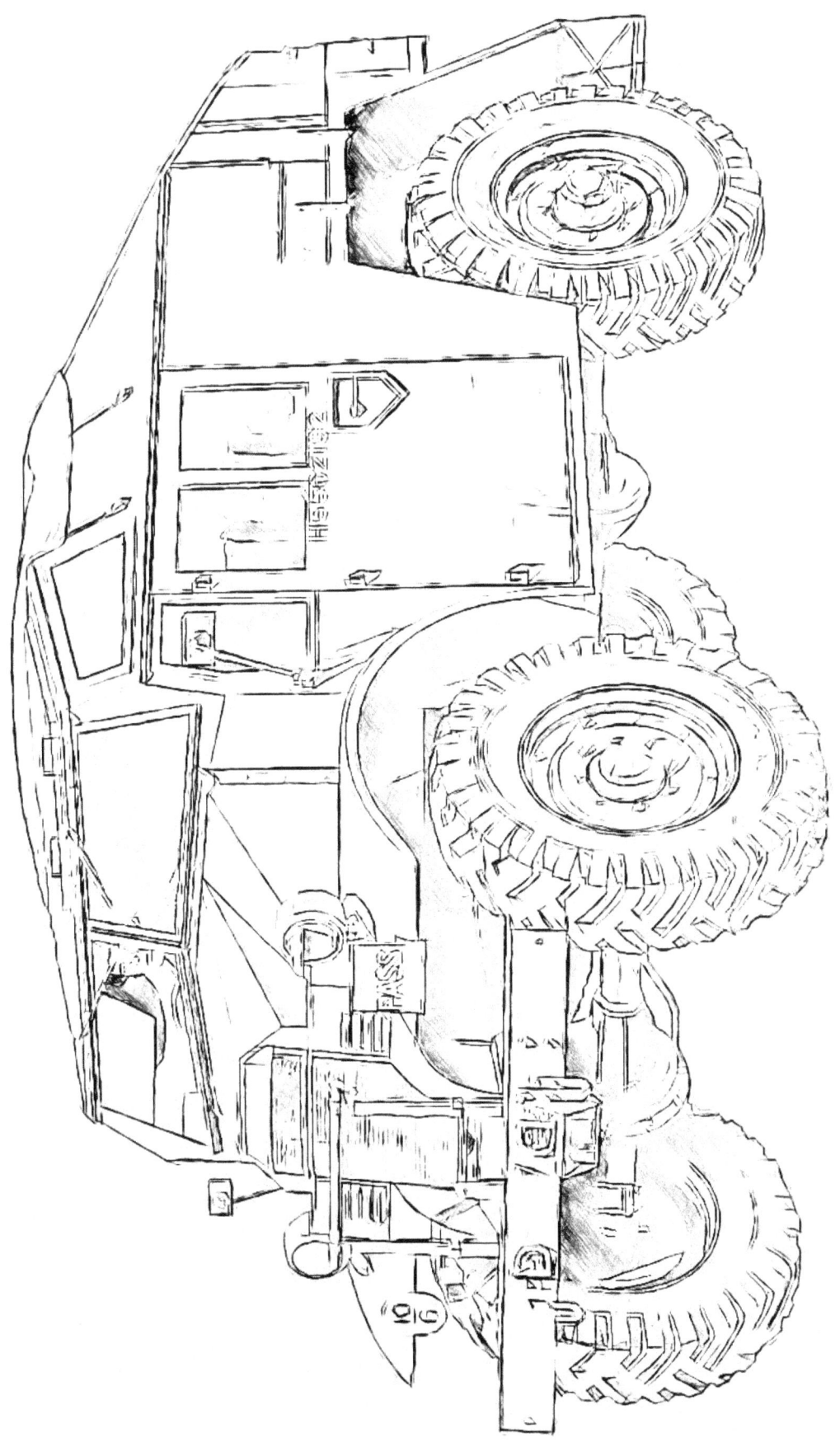

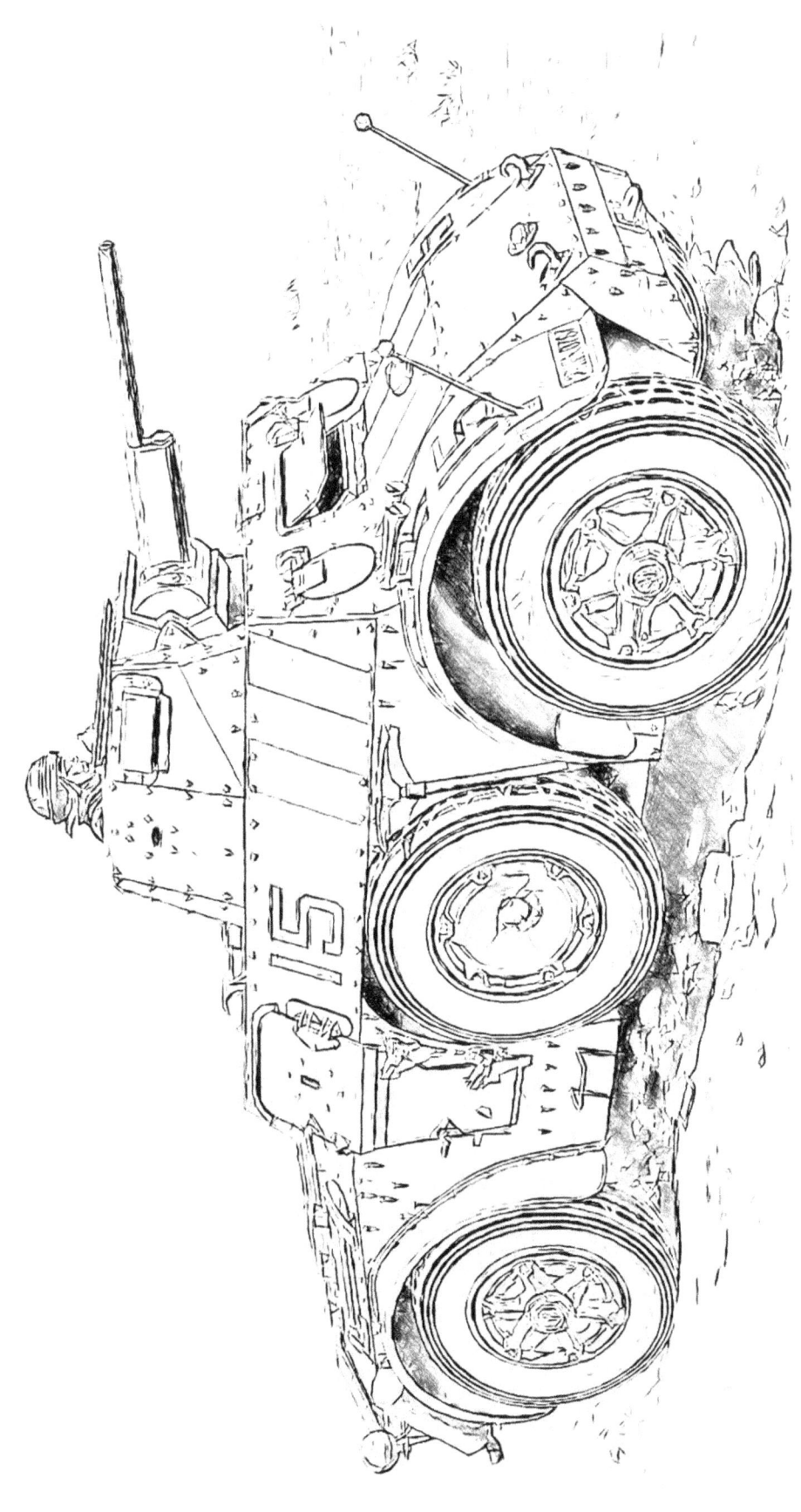

DESIGN BY

Thom Breas
First edition.
Copyright © 2020
Todos los derechos reservados.

www.ingramcontent.com/pod-product-compliance
Lightning Source LLC
Chambersburg PA
CBHW081102240526
45465CB00026B/3279